Stitching Things Together

Leah Kaminsky is a writer and physician living in Melbourne. She is a student in the MFA Fiction Writing program at Vermont College of Fine Arts, USA. She was the Eleanor Dark Flagship Fellow for Fiction in 2007 and is currently a Creative Fellow at the State Library of Victoria. She is the author of several books, and is editor of an anthology of prominent physician-writers, **The Pen and the Stethoscope** *(Scribe Publishing, 2010).*

Interactive Press
The Literature Series

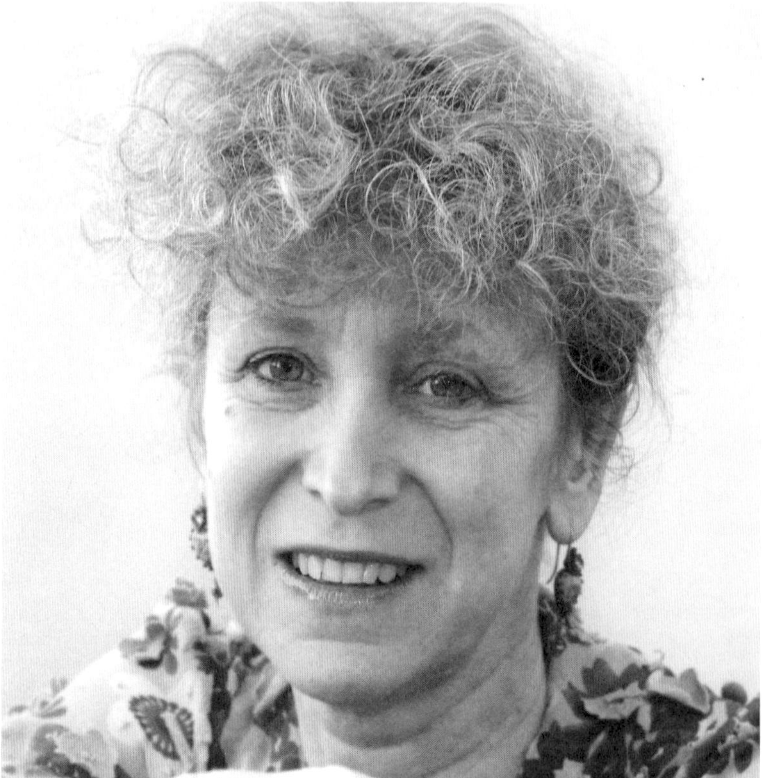

Stitching Things Together

Leah Kaminsky

Interactive Press
Brisbane

Interactive Press
an imprint of IP (Interactive Publications Pty Ltd)
Treetop Studio • 9 Kuhler Court
Carindale, Queensland, Australia 4152
sales@ipoz.biz
ipoz.biz/IP/IP.htm

First published by IP in 2010
© Leah Kaminsky, 2010

All rights reserved. Without limiting the rights under copyright reserved above, no part of this publication may be reproduced, stored in or introduced into a retrieval system, or transmitted, in any form or by any means (electronic, mechanical, photocopying, recording or otherwise), without the prior written permission of the copyright owner and the publisher of this book.

Printed in 12 pt Cochin on 14 pt Garamond Premier Pro.

National Library of Australia
Cataloguing-in-Publication entry:

Author: Kaminsky, Leah, 1959-

Title: Stitching things together / Leah Kaminsky.

ISBN: 9781921479694 (pbk.)

Subjects: Holocaust, Jewish (1939-1945)--Poetry.
          Holocaust survivors--Poetry.

Dewey Number: A821.3

for Yohanan, Alon, Ella and Maia

Acknowledgements

Front Cover Image: Marco Fink and Ella Loeffler

Jacket Design: David Reiter

Author Photo: Paul Loughnan

Some of these poems have been previously published in the following anthologies and journals:

Antipodes, *CHEST*, *Cordite Review*, *Divan*, *Fine Line*, *Forever Eve Anthology*, *Islet*, *Mattoid*, Max Harris Poetry Award 2008, *No Overalls Required*, *Poetry Australia*, *Quadrant*, *Shin Shalom Peace Competition Anthology*, *Spilt Milk-RMIT poets*, *The Australian Jewish News*, *The Envelope Please 2007* (John Shaw Neilson Award 2nd winner), *The Tin Wash Dish Anthology*, *Up the Staircase*, *Varuna Picaro Press Anthology*, and *Zest* (Australian Poetry Centre Poem of the Month, Jan 2010).

Special thanks to Peter Balakian, Peter Bishop, Jennie Fraine, Donna-Lee Frieze, Diana Hanaor, Lee Kofman, Paul Kooperman, Deborah Leiser-Moore, Sandra Levin, Les Murray, Rosemary Nissen-Wade, William Packard (dec), Ron Pretty, David Reiter and the Australian Poetry Centre Café Poet program.

Section titles of the manuscript are from *Tailoring For Women* by Gertrude Mason, A & C Black Ltd, 1935.

Contents

I: The Importance of a Well-Cut Pattern

Stitching things together, 2007	5
Dealing the cards	7
Aus(chwitz) to Aus(tralia)	9
Recipes from the SS Kitchen	12
Little Vienna Cafe, Carlisle Street, 1965	13
My father crosses Acland Street, 1987	14
Matthew Michael	16
Circle Dance (what we have learned from the past)	17
Shivering wings (of a bee)	19

II: Testing the Drafted Pattern

Letter to William Carlos Williams	23
Thalassaemia	24
How to Lumbar Puncture a Child	25
Monday morning at the Clinic	27
Orifices	28
Transplant	30
Pieces of me	32
Comfortable with the Snake	33

III: Preparation of the Material for Cutting

Hotel Belle, Hayarkon Street, Tel Aviv	37
Here and there – 1991	38
Eucalyptus dreaming	39
Yom Kippur, Gaza	40
The Circle Closes	41
Still Life with Children, Haifa 2000	43
A poem for Alon on his eighth birthday	44
The Turtle Comes up for Air	46
Days of usefulness	47
My daughter goes on camp	48
Chrysalis	49
Storm (Haifa, 2000)	50
Packing to leave	52
Mothers of War (tribute to Freydis)	53
Mr Potato Head and the Middle East Crisis	55

Stitching Things Together

I:

The Importance of a Well-Cut Pattern

Stitching things together, 2007

I: Tracing the pattern

I stab the curved needle
into broken skin
pulling edges together
with blue, nylon sutures

II: Alterations

my father was a tailor
on Haufgass in Zhetl, 1931
running his thumb
over loose threads

after he set the pigeons free on May 1st
red ribbons tied to their legs
he sat in Lushinkes gaol for months
urine poured into his Communist nostrils

my grandfather shared a bottle
of vodka with the guard
and put his son on board the *SS Moreton Bay*
in 1938, before the storm began

we sacrifice everything for our children
father said as he sewed coats in Melbourne
looking down from the window onto Flinders Lane
at men loading mannequins into trucks

while Europe blazed and swallowed up
his youth, his love, his life
he basted coat sleeves
and pad-stitched lapels

III: Pressing the Seams

local anaesthetic wears off
the laceration begins to throb
the pain of the body
split open, returns

Dealing the cards

I: Mizinek *

Fifteen years after father limped down Flinders Lane
and mother drank bromide tea in Bergen Belsen
I was born, an accident of old age
Why bring children into such a world?

I was a good girl then
my parents' little miracle
their heart and soul and hope

II: Wrestling ghosts

On Saturdays they played
Polish rummy
crammed around the kitchen table in Caulfield
with Gdale and Genia, Luba and Max

the women smoked Craven A's
the men ate greasy herring on rye
sipping whisky before they dealt

kids would wrestle in the lounge room
evil Dr Schnitzelbaum body-slammed Lewin the Jew
and I was always referee – *1,2,3, you're out!*

ghosts cheered from the sidelines
hidden behind the cigarette haze
no one ever saw them, except me

I resurrected them from the dead
their faces locked away
behind mother's eyes

and I fell into her world
wanting to be the air
that filled her every breath

III: Shock

In this house, in my room
where I dreamed for years
unspoken words piled up

father sat on the floor
playing *Go Fish* with me
his crooked leg stretched out

while electrodes forced the sun
of pre-war Poland back into mother's brain
and she saw a carp swimming in the tub

her mother chopping off its head
mincing the flesh for gefilte fish
served with a slice of carrot for shabbat

did the volts burn the darkness in her
and force my faceless relatives to move on
searching for shelter in another's haunted mind?

unspoken words piled up between us
silent, like murdered bodies
the *what-we-should-have-saids*
the *if-onlys*

* the youngest child (Yiddish)

Aus(chwitz) to Aus(tralia)

I: Aus(chwitz)

the ashes settle on the town
beached white bones huddle under snow
the ovens   the ovens
a baker's dozen
thirteen faces kneaded dough
never faced my face they gaze
in silence scream my name

from dying embers rose the smallest flame
blackened eyes watched
chimneys belching smoke
my mother's mother sisters brothers

scattered with the breeze

across the seas
my mother saw a safer shore
mother sisters brothers
she followed them as far as she could go
and hidden in the clouds
their only shroud
they rained for forty years
their bitter endless tears

II: Aus(tralia)

While Bondi's waves were crashing in the son
there lay within the oven mother's bun
pat-a-cake pat-a-cake baker's man
bake me a cake as fast as you can

sacrificial lamb
basting in the oven
she fed me spoonfuls
one by one
one for your aunt
one for your cousin
          from
the oven
          for
the ovens
          for
the baker's dozen

I spat out every mouthful
in defiance of her past

of eyes that had no face
of mouths that had no voice
and I played with my curls
like the rest of the girls
and cried that my hair wasn't straight

and in every mirror
she saw her shaven head

one day the mirror cracked
she saw her ghost had no reflection
she told me Hitler won the war
I laughed and went to bed

that evening
the empty heart stopped
bleeding
she never woke
she never spoke my name
again

the dirt has settled on her coffin
bleached white bones rest beneath

she came from god-forsaken hell

to hell
forsaken

Recipes from the SS Kitchen

mother stands beside the highchair
feeding me tomatoes
sprinkled with sugar
my first sour-sweet mouthful

she wipes stray seeds from my chin
with the edge of a bib
then offers more

shoves in spoonful after spoonful
her bony fingers brushing my cheek
here she comes again with schnitzel
gnocchi, potatoes, klops, broth

holding back the bile
she chokes on meals she never ate
the best cook in the camp

Little Vienna Cafe, Carlisle Street, 1965

what I remember most
is the waiter's bow tie
white shirt, tailored pants
horn-rimmed spectacles
and his way of serving schnitzel
as he smiled at my mother

a glass of red wine for her
raspberry cordial for me
her nails painted red
mine bitten to the quick

what I try to forget
is father spilling soup on his trousers
rubbing at the stain
with a white, linen serviette
mother glaring at him
while the waiter hovered nearby

and now I remember
trying to ignore her scowl
wishing he would hurry up
and bring sacher torte for dessert

My father crosses Acland Street, 1987

life teaches old people
the art of cheating death
it designs the wrinkles
on the blueprint
woven like an intricate rug
and carves them into stone

time tiptoes over
blank canvas
strolls across the forehead
a cat prowling
in search of prey

stop for the old Jew
he launches his size 5 feet
onto the road
the hem of his black coat
winding around his ankles

stare at the hump
on his wife's back
she steps out blindly
leaning on her stick
her head pointed down

for them there is only here
deaf to the horns
that protest their age
they plod on
focused on their shoes

only a grey notion
that somewhere ahead
lies Balberyski's Yiddish bookshop
they cannot turn around
to look at where they came from

old eyes remember
what young eyes will not see

Matthew Michael

My brother's son
lies upon our father
who art almost in heaven

with no control
of fragile frames
they howl in harmony

sphincters suddenly open
faeces, urine seeps through
soiling sheets

a mirror gazes into a mirror
blue eyes reflect blue eyes
tears for two

tears from the womb of death
tears from the womb of life
two cry as one

from the window beside my father's bed
I can see the flower stall on the corner of the street
daffodils make me think of hospitals and spring

morning rain
afternoon sun pushes back
grey clouds

tomorrow the heavens may open again and rain
upon our father
the sun will shine upon
my brother's son

Circle Dance (what we have learned from the past)

I: Them

they are the only ones left
after the storm
bodies of the drowned
lie slumped in the mud

children toss small pebbles
across receding waters
stand at the edge of pools
peering through the mist

mothers search for their first born
in the forest beyond the hill
birds must be singing there
gossiping themselves to sleep

fathers wade in knee-deep
stand tall in the centre
staring at their reflections
when the ripples still

if they wait long enough
the water curls around them
and they are able to see
the distorted dead watching them

II: Us

we have walked a long way
to reach here, you and I
so keep listening
they might speak

it may be their faces
that show you a glimpse
of our future
from their past

a crack in the stone wall of time
could reveal a different landscape
where children dance
among the wildflowers

they twirl round and round
singing the same song over again
singing the same tune
and the same pointless words

Shivering wings (of a bee)

this is the terrible hour of the hive
the massacre of the innocents

youthful queens lie in waxen prisons
royal virgins, waiting to kill
rivals still encased in silent cocoons

the way out is to press through blindly
always like this, into the light

from blindness to blindness
a circle
traced back to its beginnings

II:

Testing the Drafted Pattern

Letter to William Carlos Williams

Dr Williams, you wrote on prescription pads
your poetry rose from the droves of people
who poured past your eyes
and my eyes are raging with tears of frustration
as he and she and they and them
come in and confess abuse regret question

you were the trusted doctor poet writer
and I am the doctor poet writer
they do not trust anymore
we have lost our faith in healers
life in this room is about plumbing and pills

I sit alone at my desk
pouring poems onto an empty page
listening to the droning voice
of the lady in the waiting room
complaining about her angina and swollen legs

I am tired, lady. I am bloating with the words
of him and her and they and them
nowhere left to put them all
so they spill over into poems
you strangle me like a tight scarf
that I dream of unravelling one day

Thalassaemia

sitting at the back of a lecture theatre
haematology 303
he spoke of thalassaemia
we dreamed of an imaginary Greek isle
scribbles on the board blurred into chalk dust
white sand on a beach
and words flapped like seagulls around the room
we whispered dreams of our island Thalassaemia
and snuck out through the exit door
sailing off to sunset at the pub

Nikolou
the blood drips steadily from the vein
on the back of your hand
a little Greek isle
alone in a sea of disease

How to Lumbar Puncture a Child

let the nurses bring it in and hold it down
don't let its mother into the room
don't smile or say hello

stand aside
stare out the window
blue sky above
carpark below

don't look into its eyes
don't listen to its screams
don't touch its fevered face

wash your fingers clean
put on the gown
mask over your mouth
gloves on your hands

place the drape over its back
stare only at the square
of flesh exposed

take the needle from the tray
first stab a bullseye
if the spinal fluid drips out steadily
crystal clear

collect each drop
fill three yellow tubes
bandaid over the hole

remove your gown
remove your gloves
remove your mask
wash your hands

turn around
walk out the door
don't look back

Monday morning at the Clinic

Lonely Merle and her swollen legs are back again
I open and close my wooden jaw
a ventriloquist's dummy wearing a stethoscope
someone else's words emerge

In return, Merle speaks lovingly of her sherry
and of her duck who bit the district nurse
and of the dance contest
she won in nineteen fifty nine
at the Maison Deluxe
now a café filled with trendies
spilling out onto the footpath

they reluctantly move their chairs
to let her wheelchair pass
barely lifting their eyes
from the Entertainment Guide

Orifices

I stare into them every day
swab, prod, examine them with torches
syringe and scrape
some days I feel like I could disappear into their depths
gasping, human holes
pustular, purulent and perverse

Pupils, soul windows, bottomless pits
I have fallen into
on better days
now reveal their network of criss-crossing
crumbling, blood snakes
I shine my light on their blind spot.

Ears, blocked to the outside world
mostly not hearing
not listening
deafened by wax
and wane
I blast them with my spray

Nostrils, oceans of snot
mucousy, green seas at high tide
spilling onto Kleenex shores
olfactory numbness to the stench outside
I plunge my oar-swab into their depths
and bring fresh air

Mouths, gaping Luna parks
uvulas dangling down midline
like useless, red penises
my tongue depressor
makes them gag
and vomit up their truths

Belly buttons, the final wrench from mother
filled with lint and disrespect
a halfway house of masturbation
I leave them well alone
not true orifices anymore
but walled-off wounds of birth

Vulvas with clam-like fronds
greedy and desirous
they flap in the wind
swallow my speculum with ease
or freeze like cold, stunned mullets
guarding the gates

And sweet, little bum holes
my favourite
closed to the world
winking with honesty
that shit lies
behind every turn

Transplant

the widow of the dead man
gave his heart away
before she became a widow

she signed the form
and they turned off
the switch

the dead man
lost his heart
before he became
a dead man

they tore it out
and gave it to
the dying man

the dying man lived
with the heart
of the dead man
and wrote to thank the widow

the widow followed
the dead man's heart
to the dying man

and fell in love
with the dying man
who carried
the dead man's heart

the dead man's heart
broke one day
and the dying man died

leaving a widowed
heart

Pieces of me

I begin to forget myself
climb out of my skin
turn it inside out like a coat
and drape it over a chair

I am leaving this place
this room where the voices call
help me, mend me

I disconnect the phone
doodle on prescription pads
make shopping lists

I begin to forget myself
edging slowly towards the door
as they remain fixed in their seats
talking talking talking their ills

and after they undress
waiting for me on the couch
I slip outside

I am walking away today
down to the sea and the sand
peeling off my white coat, like dead skin
sacrificing it to the waves

Comfortable with the Snake

I am getting comfortable with the snake on my left
and the centaur on my right
stars roll around, changing roles
scorpio dies, orion comes to life
birds twitter by day, but hidden under leaves
they watch me rise at night

In jewelled slippers, I tiptoe across the sky
he searches from below, through his telescope
alone in the observatory
I stride now, talking to peacocks, flies, dolphins
swimming, flying across the night air
dip my hands into the Jewel Box

He is looking for nebulas, giant nebulas
as I sift through the fabric of the night sky
he plots the axis of alpha centauri
I bounce along the craters of the moon
he determines the coordinates of the sea of tranquillity
I wade through the celestial river

I am the blonde, he is my shadow
calculates through all my dreams
the hunter and the dogs look down
watching him in the tin shed
as he checks the charts and measures
staring up through prisms

He does not see me
plans his next move
how many degrees
narrowing his gaze
as I leap from star to star
in the black seaweed sky

III:

Preparation of the Material for Cutting

Hotel Belle, Hayarkon Street, Tel Aviv

nothing great about Hotel Belle
she stands on the corner
of the street where the girls
in their tight-fitting tasselled tops
sit in doorways of ramshackle flats
across from the fountain in the square
where policemen walk the beat

walk further, twelve steps for you
twenty for me, to the shop where
an old Jew sells paintings of kitsch
next door to Doctor Lick, where the
ice-cream cools the frozen tongues
of the girls who come between customers

late November, late at night
we walked along the beach where waves
fell like whales dumped on shore
we walked some more and shared a Coke
in a deserted café

in summer we open the door just enough to smell
the musty air of Hotel Belle
curling her fingers around our hands

Here and there – 1991

for Nani

he winks from behind a gas mask
dog on his lap trembling
scuds whiz over Haifa

5 hours drive to Baghdad from here
500km wouldn't get me far past Albury
on the Hume - I've done it several times

this poem for him has no rhyme
or reason. It is for his junk, white undies
old postcards, Beatles' White Album

we survive because of woodpeckers
mongooses, Palestinian sunbirds
and gossipy bulbul birds

remembering the baby kookaburra
with a broken blue wing
he saved on that Port Fairy road

Eucalyptus dreaming

The trees here aren't my trees
they are my mother's
and her mother's
the woodpecker is not my bird
it taps out foreign tunes
not kookaburra, magpie, currawong

I would hug a gum
leave seeds out for lorikeets
shoo the blowflies from my face

the bulbul bird is singing in the carob
the barn owl hoots at night in the pine
gum blood flows in me

close my eyes and I am paddling
in a stream near Nourlangie Rock
spying on magpie geese and Jesus birds

the trees here aren't my trees
they grow on my mother's roots
and I am a ghost gum

Yom Kippur, Gaza

Island of joy, she stands alone
one year since the waters broke

passing moons, smile like clowns
I cannot catch them as they spin

she clings to a chair, takes three steps
pushing from baby feet, raises hands skyward

points to the stilled child on the TV screen
slumped onto his father's lap

The Circle Closes

I: Leaving Melbourne, 1991

the day a *hamsin* blew
across from the East
you brought me home to Haifa
and closed the bedroom door

with first light
you watched me wake
and spoke my weary name
the imprint of my heart heavy on the bed

I left my father behind, unable to speak
his eyes already on that ancient journey
I left the 60s lace, the 70s trim, the 80s zips
he sewed onto me, patched together with love
I left my home, the pattern cut in two
torn between far away and further

I turned and stepped aside
into my life, towards you
spiders wove their webs
in corners of our house on Sea Road
while cyclamens unfurled in our garden
father died alone

II: Living in Haifa, 1999

one *Shabbat* we drove up to Dalyat-al-Carmel
past the falafel stalls, jars of crimson pickles
the sweet baklava shop, the smell of honey in the air
and out along the road to the *mukhraka*
where, looking out over boulders of memory and time
my knitted coat frayed at the seams

I am imported goods
tattooed with the history of war
born in Yiddish, the *oy gevalt*s of parents
who pushed me into life

I trace the veins in my legs
that criss-cross up to the delta of my thighs
I have delivered three children
into this land

the places that used to hurt
like a scream held back
have crumbled inwards now
silent as a heartbeat

I have become an acrobat
balancing on piles of the dead
I am a buckle
in the circle of names
the barren daughter
who surrendered to love

Still Life with Children, Haifa 2000

this is the poem of cooking spaghetti
before the kids get home
and dump their bags in the kitchen

the baby asleep on the couch
while the printer drones
out lousy drafts

about jet planes overhead
bombs in Tel Aviv and Netanya
this is the poem of not writing poems

on a Tuesday at eleven in a cafe
that is bombed by five
(home washing dishes instead)

this is the poem of poems waiting inside
like my three small eggs
suspended for years, until one moment
of love, passion or madness

A poem for Alon on his eighth birthday

And so this is a poem for you
although you write it yourself
every day
when you look for your soccer ball
and kick it around the house
last month, you broke an antique plate

Holes in your socks
eyes on TV or computer screen
you know all the words of
Popeye and Pokemon
the jingles of every ad
you sing them out loud behind a closed toilet door

You turn eight
and ten years of Haifa sun
have burnt my eyes
another ten and you will carry a gun
I stare into your ocean eyes
they are too deep for a boy

I want to stop you now
keep you close, bound to me
watch you play Aussie Rules
delete from you lexicon
intifada, bomb shelter
gas mask, dead baby

for your birthday, I would stop the sirens
that call the whole country to attention
drivers on the freeway, stand beside their cars
a minute's silence
in memory of all the eighteen year old
soldiers killed

I will tie a ribbon around this poem
and put it in my drawer for ten years
then I will give you
a poem for Alon on his eighteenth birthday

The Turtle Comes up for Air

every few minutes it stretches its neck
extends its ancient head from its shell
breaks through the surface
like my son's penis as he lies in the bath

when I look, he withdraws under the
waterline. I pretend not to see
the flag at full mast. It is Independence Day
there will be fireworks tonight

my son gets dressed slowly
dribbles his soccer ball
from his bedroom to the kitchen,
takes out a cucumber, and eats it whole

The season is wrong for our red-eared slider
it likes humidity and warmth
I make faces through the aquarium
it stares back and does not blink
five webbed toes splayed on the glass

Days of usefulness

(Haifa, intifada 1999)

the hair I pull out of her pink comb
holds a pearly egg, clinging to the shaft
she examines it between finger and thumb
then I douse her with vinegar

she smells like salad dressing most days
anointed every night this week
and as she steps out of the bath
tiny corpses spiral down the drain

tomorrow there will be a school drill
she will sit in the bomb shelter
beside her brother, who shoots Pokemons
while she reads about the lion and the thorn

My daughter goes on camp

The door of my house
stands open
and I am carrying
her suitcase out

her toy rabbit stashed
at the bottom of her bag
marshmallows, a half a loaf of bread
I drive her to the station

standing on the platform
watching her watching me
through the window of the train
the dread of some other place
swallows me

I am a woman who lives
in the places I dream of at night
my daughter's face framed
in a blurred old photo

when will I know quiet joy?
when will school camp be school camp
a train just a train, an oven just an oven?
when will I let them go
knowing they will come back?

she waves her hand
fighting through mists of time
to reach me as the train pulls away
saying goodbye to the living
while I am busy waking up the dead

Chrysalis

She is casting off
her old cocoon
of too-small clothes
left around the house

I reach out to hold her close
against the breasts
that helped her grow
my days of motheruse now gone

the clock ticks away the years
since I sewed back Bun Bun's ear
I show her an old bib
wave it like a bullfighter

we used to walk hand in hand
she was the moth around my flame
now that she is grown
I can see my death hovering

she is casting off
her old cocoon
as she should, showing off
shiny wings to the boys

Storm (Haifa, 2000)

I: Truth

thunder groans for hours
sending out flashes of day
into night

morning
forces clouds away
bringing sunshine centre stage

a trendy couple move next door
smashing interior walls
tossing out someone else's life

I have come to save the past
collecting history
from sidewalk junk

II: Lies

when my son was four
he drew long legs dangling
off my circle head

two arms, scribble hair
shoes firmly on both feet
his faceless mother floating

his father filled the page
with zigzag mouth
and spiral eyes

our heads, Venn diagrams
limbs overlapping
piercing hollow hearts

III: Truth

I wake from the night
to the swell of blood tide
my womb curling in on itself

I know anatomy
the name of every artery
filled with aching clots

jet fighters fly overhead
old men point to Mars
the earth cuddles dead soldiers

one was a daisy-child
plucked and tossed into mud
honey dripping from wounds

his blood spilled for bees
cries unheard
in the wilderness of loss

Packing to leave

You sit on top of the wardrobe
waiting for this moment
then shower a year's worth
of dust in my eyes

you let me unzip you slowly
like a lover, you open out
ready to be filled
underpants, toothpaste, bras
deodorant, tampons
koala souvenirs, boomerangs

I am taking you back
TLV BKK MLB
I lug parts of myself
around inside you
seesawing north and south
over the fulcrum of an equator
which is becoming too tight
for this earth's midriff bulge

we are growing old
the earth, my suitcase and I
fraying at our seams
well travelled, weary
looking forward to departure
longing for return

Mothers of War (tribute to Freydis)

the mothers of war
glomesh goddesses
show their breasts to the world

the mothers of war
pregnant and proud
carry the seeds of their dead sons

the mothers of war
lay eggs
in barbed wire nests

the mothers of war
legs splayed apart
fire cannonball babies into the night

the mothers of war
bite through the cord with steel teeth
the placenta lies on a dish on the bench

the mothers of war
awake to the cries of their sons
in the dead of the night

the mothers of war
raise bottles and pour
swords down their dead sons' throats

the mothers of war
shelter their sons in their arms
and sing songs to the crying brave

the mothers of war
sit in the fire, and knit
as their sons chop down trees outside

the mothers of war
march through the maze of trench-dreams
knee-deep in the blood of their sons

the mothers of war
bear weapons
slapping their breasts with the swords of their sons

Mr Potato Head and the Middle East Crisis

ZAKA – members of this organisation, most of whom are Orthodox Jews, aid in the identification of the victims of terrorism and other disasters, gathering body parts and spilled blood for proper burial.

the blast tore his body apart
they found his left arm on Hechalutz Street
his right foot on Ha'atzmaut
and his hat, corner Herzl and Nevi'im

they came from ZAKA to piece him back together
those pious men with beards and sidecurls
a mitzvah* so holy to bury him whole
they placed bits of liver into zip-lock bags

when he was new
body parts would hold tight
no crushed ribs or squeaky joints
nowadays his feet are bound with tape

they couldn't find all of him
so they went downtown
to the toyshop near Suidan's bakery
and asked for spare parts

Abu Musa rummaged through an old box
of noses, ears and smiles
and kindly donated
a moustache to the cause

at the funeral Potato Head stood one-eyed
on the child's freshly dug grave
and wished they made accessory tears
he could slot inside his plastic heart

*mitzvah – good deed

Recent IP Poetry

Ruin, Roberta Lowing
ISBN 9781921479434, AU$25

In Defence of Hawaiian Shirts, B N Oakman
ISBN 9781921479410, AU$25

Wings of the Same Bird, Lorraine McGuigan
ISBN 9781921479359, AU$25

Stepping Over Seasons, Ashley Capes
ISBN 9781921479328, AU$25

Towards a Grammar of Being, Julie Waugh
ISBN 9781921479243, AU$25

Voyagers, Mark Pirie and Tim Jones
ISBN 9781921479221, AU$25.95

Liquefaction, Iain Britton
ISBN 9781921479175, AU$25

In Between the Dancing, E. A. Gleeson
ISBN 9781921479106, AU$25

Invaders of the Heart, Lee Knowles
ISBN 9781921479090, AU$25

The Possibility of Flight, Lia Hills
ISBN 9781921479076, AU$25

For the latest from IP, please visit us online at
http://ipoz.biz/Store/Store.htm
or contact us by **phone/fax** at *61 7 3324 9319* or *61 7 3395 0269*
or sales@ipoz.biz